# EARTHQUAKES

BY PETER MURRAY

Published by The Child's World®
1980 Lookout Drive • Mankato, MN 56003-1705
800-599-READ • www.childsworld.com

ACKNOWLEDGMENTS
The Child's World®: Mary Berendes, Publishing Director
Olivia Gregory: Editing

ISBN 9781631437649
LCCN 2014945414

Printed in the United States of America
Mankato, MN
November, 2014
PA02245

## ABOUT THE AUTHOR

Peter Murray has written more than 80 children's books on science, nature, history, and other topics. He also writes novels for adults and teens under the name Pete Hautman. An animal lover, Peter lives in Golden Valley, Minnesota, in a house with one woman, two poodles, several dozen spiders, thousands of microscopic dust mites, and an occasional mouse.

# Table of Contents

# Earthquake!

**The cause of earthquakes was first stated in 1760 by a British scientist named John Michell.**

**Earthquakes even happen on the moon! These are called "moonquakes."**

On January 17, 1994, the people of Los Angeles, California woke up at exactly 4:31 A.M. The ground was shaking, and so were the houses and buildings. Dishes fell from cupboards, and bookcases crashed to the floor. Every car alarm in the city started howling. Gas lines and water pipes were torn open. People ran from their homes, afraid that their ceilings would collapse. What caused all of this? An earthquake!

Earthquakes happen every day, all over the world. Let's learn more about how and why they happen.

*This apartment building was destroyed in the 1994 California earthquake.*

# Inside Earth

To understand earthquakes, you need to learn about Earth itself. Beneath our feet lies Earth's **crust**, a layer of cool, hard rock. It is about 60 miles (97 km) thick. The crust is made up of huge pieces, or **crustal plates**. Each crustal plate is thousands of miles across. The plates fit together like pieces of a jigsaw puzzle.

Beneath Earth's crust lies a layer of hot, melted rock called the **mantle**. The crustal plates float along on the gooey mantle, pushing against one another and pulling apart. They move so slowly that they might take a hundred years to travel an inch. Sometimes, though, they move a little faster.

When crustal plates pull apart or press together, tremendous forces build up. Sometimes the plates slip and move so suddenly that we can feel the earth shift beneath our feet. When the earth moves suddenly and violently like this, we call it an earthquake.

*The top photo shows Earth's crustal plates. The bottom photo shows what's inside Earth.*

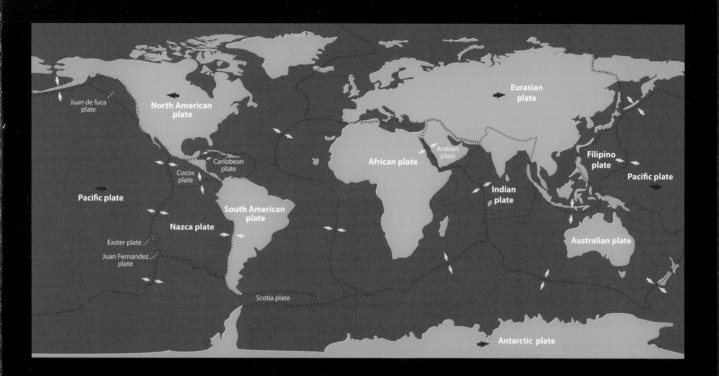

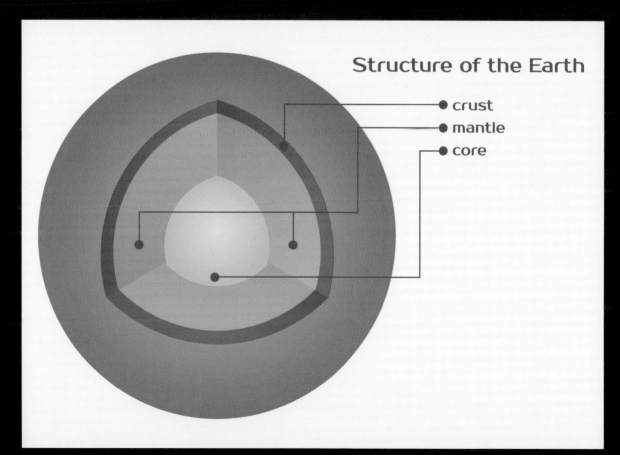

## Structure of the Earth

● crust
● mantle
● core

# Faults

The plates of the San Andreas Fault usually only move about 2 inches (5 cm) a year. This is about as fast as your fingernails grow!

Scientists estimate that if the California plates continue to move at their current pace, Los Angeles and San Francisco will be next to each other in about 15 million years.

A **fault** is a crack in Earth's crust. Most faults occur where the crustal plates meet. The San Andreas Fault in California lies between the Pacific Ocean plate and the North American plate.

Most faults are hidden deep underground. Others lie deep under the ocean where we cannot see them. The San Andreas Fault is different. It reaches all the way to Earth's surface where we can see it every day.

*Here you can see the San Andreas Fault in California's Carrizo Plain.*

9

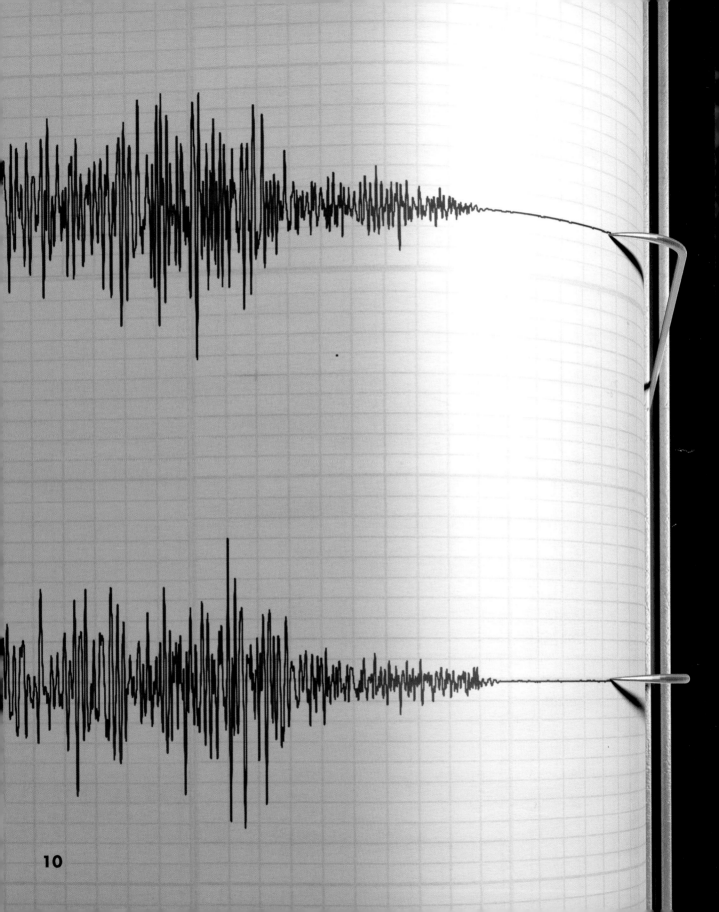

# Predicting Quakes

Scientists use machines called **seismographs** (SYZ-muh-grafs) to measure tiny movements in the earth's crust. These machines are very sensitive. In fact, a seismograph in Kansas can feel an earthquake in Los Angeles! Seismographs and other instruments help us learn more about what lies beneath our feet.

By using seismographs located in different parts of the world, scientists can tell where an earthquake started. This starting point is called the **epicenter**. Usually, the worst damage is directly above the epicenter.

In the Los Angeles earthquake of 1994, the epicenter was directly below the suburb of Northridge. Damage from the quake spread for many miles, but Northridge suffered the worst destruction. One apartment building collapsed, burying 16 people. A freeway buckled and twisted and fell apart. In nearby San Fernando, an oil pipe exploded, destroying dozens of buildings.

**The earliest type of seismograph was developed in 1751.**

**Most earthquakes occur at less than 50 miles (80 km) from the surface.**

**Far underneath the epicenter is the "hypocenter," where the fault begins.**

*The red lines on this seismograph machine show earthquake activity.*

# Earthquake Damage

When water sloshes out of a swimming pool during an earthquake, it is called a "seiche" (SAYSH).

A quake hit San Francisco, California in 1906. A terrible fire resulted, which spread through the city. The fire did far more damage than the quake itself!

Most earthquakes do little or no damage. Each year about 500,000 small earthquakes happen around the world. Luckily, only a few cause serious damage.

People who live in areas with lots of earthquakes get used to these small, harmless movements of the ground. But they never stop worrying about the big ones!

*Here you can see the damage and fire following the San Francisco earthquake of 1906.*

# Strong and Weak

One of the strongest earthquakes ever recorded struck Anchorage, Alaska in 1964. The Kenai Peninsula—including the entire town of Anchorage—sank seven feet (2 m). The area just to the south was raised by as much as ten feet (3 m). The Anchorage quake measured 8.5 on the **Richter Scale.** The Richter Scale is a way of estimating the strength of an earthquake.

The weakest earthquakes we can feel measure about 2 on the Richter Scale. These quakes often cause little damage. But anything over 6 is considered a strong earthquake. The Los Angeles earthquake of 1994 measured 6.5 on the Richter Scale.

*This part of an Anchorage street sank by several feet following the 1964 earthquake.*

# Other Problems

A tsunami and a tidal wave are two different things. Tsunamis are caused by earthquakes. Tidal waves are caused by tides.

A powerful tsunami occurred in the Indian Ocean on December 26, 2004. As many as 280,000 people died in the countries of Indonesia, India, Thailand, and Sri Lanka.

Besides destroying homes, roads, and buildings, strong earthquakes can cause other problems. They can cause avalanches and cracks in the earth. But the deadliest effects of earthquakes are giant waves of water called **tsunamis** (soo-NAM-eez).

Tsunamis are caused when a crustal plate beneath the ocean suddenly rises or falls. This quick movement creates enormous waves that travel up to 100 miles (161 km) an hour. As tsunamis approach land, they grow larger. When the waves break onto the shore, they can destroy buildings, flood roads, and even drown people. Tsunamis are very dangerous.

*The word "tsunami" in Japanese means "harbor wave."*

# Staying Safe

If an earthquake strikes, the safest place to be is outside. Outside there are fewer things that could fall on you, such as bookshelves, windows, or walls. If an earthquake happens while you are outside, go to an open area and stay there. Watch out for fallen power lines and broken glass.

If you are inside during an earthquake, take cover underneath a table or desk. Never run outside if the earthquake is already happening—you can get hurt from falling items. When the shaking stops, make your way outside to an open area. Be sure to stay away from buildings and walls. Earthquakes are often followed by smaller quakes called **aftershocks**. Aftershocks can cause weakened buildings to collapse.

**Your family should have a safety plan in place before an earthquake strikes. That way, you'll know what to do during an actual quake.**

**Stay away from windows and other glass during a quake.**

*These people are sleeping outside after an earthquake in China. The aftershocks made it unsafe to go back inside.*

**Some scientists think The Big One will happen in the next 30 years.**

In California people talk about "The Big One." The Big One is an earthquake that hasn't happened yet. It's the earthquake everyone fears will happen when forces building along the San Andreas Fault suddenly give way.

No one knows for sure what the future will bring. There may not be another major earthquake for years— or The Big One might happen tomorrow! Scientists are watching their seismographs very closely. They hope that some day they will be able to warn people before dangerous earthquakes occur.

*California has lots of cities and people. The Big One is likely to cause major damage and lots of injuries.*

# Glossary

**aftershock (AF-tur-shok)**
An aftershock is a smaller earthquake that occurs after a large one.

**crust (KRUST)**
The outer shell of Earth is called the crust. Earth's crust is about 60 miles (97 km) thick.

**crustal plates (KRUS-tul PLAYTS)**
The huge sections of Earth's crust are called crustal plates. The crustal plates fit together like a jigsaw puzzle.

**epicenter (EP-ih-sen-tur)**
The epicenter of an earthquake is the place where the quake started. The worst damage usually occurs at the epicenter.

**fault (FAWLT)**
A fault is a crack in Earth's crust. The San Andreas Fault is a huge fault in California.

**mantle (MAN-tull)**
The mantle is a layer of hot, melted rock underneath Earth's crust. The crustal plates float on the mantle.

**Richter Scale (RIK-tur SKAYL)**
The Richter Scale is a way of estimating how strong an earthquake is.

**seismograph (SYZ-muh-graf)**
Seismographs are machines that detect and measure tiny movements of the earth's crust.

**tsunamis (soo-NAM-eez)**
Tsunamis are huge waves that are created by earthquakes. Tsunamis can be very destructive.

# To Find Out More

## In the Library

Furgang, Kathy. *Everything Volcanoes and Earthquakes.* Washington, D.C.: National Geographic, 2013.

Levine, Ellen. *If You Lived at the Time of the Great San Francisco Earthquake.* New York: Scholastic, 1992.

Stiefel, Chana. *Tsunamis.* New York: Children's Press, 2009.

Than, Ker. *Earthquakes.* New York: Children's Press, 2009.

## On the Web

Visit our Web site for links about earthquakes:
**www.childsworld.com/links**

*Note to Parents, Teachers, and Librarians: We routinely check our Web links to make sure they're safe, active sites—so encourage your readers to check them out!*

# Index